50 Lunchbox Love Dishes

By: Kelly Johnson

Table of Contents

- Chicken Caesar Wrap
- Veggie Hummus Sandwich
- Turkey and Avocado Roll-Ups
- Quinoa Salad
- Mini Pita Pockets
- Egg Salad Sandwich
- Caprese Skewers
- Rice Paper Rolls
- Chicken and Rice Stir-Fry
- Greek Salad
- Pasta Salad
- BLT Wrap
- Veggie Quesadilla
- Mini Muffin Tin Frittatas
- Hummus and Veggie Wrap
- Tuna Salad
- Avocado and Tomato Sandwich
- Turkey and Cheese Roll-Ups
- Pesto Pasta
- Smashed Chickpea Salad Sandwich
- Apple and Peanut Butter Slices
- Chicken Salad Lettuce Wraps
- Veggie and Cream Cheese Roll-Ups
- Bento Box with Rice, Veggies, and Fruit
- Mini Meatballs and Marinara
- Sweet Potato and Black Bean Burrito
- Baked Chicken Tenders
- Spinach and Feta Wrap
- Fruit Salad with Yogurt
- Mini Pizzas
- Chicken and Veggie Skewers
- Roasted Veggie and Quinoa Bowl
- Almond Butter and Banana Sandwich
- Shrimp and Avocado Salad
- Grilled Cheese and Tomato Soup

- Veggie Stir-Fry with Tofu
- Pulled Pork Sliders
- Eggplant Parmesan Bites
- Salmon Salad
- Whole Wheat Pita with Cucumber and Yogurt
- Apple and Cheese Slices
- Chicken Lettuce Cups
- Zucchini Fritters
- Veggie Sushi Rolls
- Roasted Chickpeas and Veggies
- Cottage Cheese with Fruit
- Carrot and Cucumber Sticks with Dip
- Avocado and Bean Wrap
- Turkey and Spinach Pinwheels
- Pasta with Pesto and Veggies

Chicken Caesar Wrap

Ingredients:

- 2 large flour tortillas
- 2 cups cooked chicken breast (shredded or diced)
- 1 cup romaine lettuce (chopped)
- 1/4 cup grated Parmesan cheese
- 1/4 cup Caesar dressing
- Optional: Croutons (crushed)

Instructions:

1. **Prepare the Filling:** In a bowl, mix chicken, lettuce, Parmesan cheese, and Caesar dressing. Toss until evenly coated.
2. **Assemble the Wraps:** Lay a tortilla flat and spoon the mixture into the center. Add crushed croutons if desired.
3. **Roll and Serve:** Fold in the sides, roll tightly, and slice in half. Serve immediately or wrap in foil for later.

Veggie Hummus Sandwich

Ingredients:

- 2 slices of whole-grain bread
- 2 tablespoons hummus
- 1/4 cup cucumber slices
- 1/4 cup shredded carrots
- 1/4 cup spinach leaves
- 2 slices tomato

Instructions:

1. **Spread Hummus:** Spread hummus on both slices of bread.
2. **Layer Vegetables:** On one slice, layer cucumber, carrots, spinach, and tomato.
3. **Assemble and Serve:** Top with the other slice of bread, cut in half, and serve.

Turkey and Avocado Roll-Ups

Ingredients:

- 4 slices turkey breast
- 1 avocado (sliced)
- 4 lettuce leaves
- 4 small whole-grain tortillas

Instructions:

1. **Prepare the Tortilla:** Lay a tortilla flat and place a lettuce leaf on it.
2. **Add Fillings:** Top with turkey and avocado slices.
3. **Roll and Serve:** Roll tightly, slice into bite-sized pieces if desired, and serve.

Quinoa Salad

Ingredients:

- 1 cup cooked quinoa
- 1/2 cup cherry tomatoes (halved)
- 1/4 cup diced cucumber
- 1/4 cup crumbled feta cheese
- 2 tablespoons olive oil
- 1 tablespoon lemon juice
- Salt and pepper to taste

Instructions:

1. **Combine Ingredients:** In a large bowl, mix quinoa, tomatoes, cucumber, and feta cheese.
2. **Dress the Salad:** Drizzle with olive oil and lemon juice, then toss well.
3. **Season and Serve:** Season with salt and pepper, and serve chilled.

Mini Pita Pockets

Ingredients:

- 4 mini pita pockets
- 1 cup shredded lettuce
- 1/2 cup diced cucumber
- 1/2 cup diced chicken or chickpeas
- 1/4 cup tzatziki sauce

Instructions:

1. **Prepare the Filling:** In a bowl, combine lettuce, cucumber, and chicken or chickpeas. Toss with tzatziki sauce.
2. **Fill the Pitas:** Carefully open the pita pockets and fill them with the mixture.
3. **Serve:** Serve immediately or refrigerate for later.

Egg Salad Sandwich

Ingredients:

- 4 hard-boiled eggs (chopped)
- 2 tablespoons mayonnaise
- 1 teaspoon mustard
- 1/4 teaspoon salt
- 1/4 teaspoon pepper
- 2 slices of bread

Instructions:

1. **Make the Egg Salad:** In a bowl, mix chopped eggs, mayonnaise, mustard, salt, and pepper.
2. **Assemble the Sandwich:** Spread the egg salad on one slice of bread and top with the other.
3. **Serve:** Cut in half and serve.

Caprese Skewers

Ingredients:

- 12 cherry tomatoes
- 12 small mozzarella balls
- 12 fresh basil leaves
- 2 tablespoons balsamic glaze

Instructions:

1. **Assemble Skewers:** Thread a tomato, mozzarella ball, and basil leaf onto a toothpick or skewer. Repeat until all ingredients are used.
2. **Drizzle and Serve:** Drizzle with balsamic glaze and serve as an appetizer or snack.

Rice Paper Rolls

Ingredients:

- 8 rice paper sheets
- 1 cup cooked shrimp or tofu (sliced)
- 1 cup julienned vegetables (carrots, cucumber, bell peppers)
- 1/4 cup cilantro leaves
- Dipping sauce (peanut or soy sauce)

Instructions:

1. **Soften Rice Paper:** Dip each rice paper sheet in warm water until soft, then lay flat on a clean surface.
2. **Add Fillings:** Place shrimp or tofu, vegetables, and cilantro in the center.
3. **Roll and Serve:** Fold in the sides, roll tightly, and serve with dipping sauce.

Chicken and Rice Stir-Fry

Ingredients:

- 2 cups cooked rice
- 1 cup cooked chicken (diced)
- 1 cup mixed vegetables (carrots, peas, bell peppers)
- 2 tablespoons soy sauce
- 1 tablespoon sesame oil
- 1 clove garlic (minced)

Instructions:

1. **Sauté Vegetables:** In a large pan or wok, heat sesame oil and sauté garlic until fragrant. Add vegetables and cook until tender.
2. **Add Chicken and Rice:** Stir in chicken and rice, mixing well.
3. **Season and Serve:** Add soy sauce, stir well, and serve hot.

Greek Salad

Ingredients:

- 2 cups chopped romaine lettuce
- 1 cup cherry tomatoes (halved)
- 1/2 cup cucumber (sliced)
- 1/4 cup red onion (thinly sliced)
- 1/4 cup Kalamata olives
- 1/4 cup feta cheese (crumbled)
- 2 tablespoons olive oil
- 1 tablespoon red wine vinegar
- 1 teaspoon oregano
- Salt and pepper to taste

Instructions:

1. **Assemble Salad:** In a large bowl, combine lettuce, tomatoes, cucumber, onion, olives, and feta.
2. **Make Dressing:** In a small bowl, whisk olive oil, vinegar, oregano, salt, and pepper.
3. **Toss and Serve:** Pour dressing over the salad, toss well, and serve.

Pasta Salad

Ingredients:

- 2 cups cooked pasta (e.g., rotini or penne)
- 1/2 cup cherry tomatoes (halved)
- 1/2 cup diced cucumber
- 1/4 cup diced bell peppers
- 1/4 cup shredded mozzarella cheese
- 2 tablespoons Italian dressing

Instructions:

1. **Mix Ingredients:** Combine cooked pasta, vegetables, and cheese in a large bowl.
2. **Add Dressing:** Pour Italian dressing over the mixture and toss well.
3. **Chill and Serve:** Refrigerate for at least 30 minutes before serving.

BLT Wrap

Ingredients:

- 2 large tortillas
- 4 slices cooked bacon
- 1 cup chopped lettuce
- 1/2 cup diced tomatoes
- 2 tablespoons mayonnaise

Instructions:

1. **Prepare Wraps:** Spread mayonnaise over each tortilla.
2. **Add Fillings:** Layer bacon, lettuce, and tomatoes on top.
3. **Roll and Serve:** Roll tightly, slice in half, and serve.

Veggie Quesadilla

Ingredients:

- 2 large tortillas
- 1 cup shredded cheese (cheddar or Monterey Jack)
- 1/4 cup diced bell peppers
- 1/4 cup diced onions
- 1/4 cup corn kernels

Instructions:

1. **Heat Tortilla:** Place one tortilla in a hot skillet.
2. **Add Fillings:** Sprinkle cheese, vegetables, and more cheese on top. Cover with the second tortilla.
3. **Cook and Flip:** Cook until the cheese melts, flip, and cook the other side until golden brown.
4. **Serve:** Slice into wedges and serve with salsa or sour cream.

Mini Muffin Tin Frittatas

Ingredients:

- 6 eggs
- 1/2 cup diced vegetables (e.g., spinach, bell peppers, onions)
- 1/4 cup shredded cheese
- Salt and pepper to taste

Instructions:

1. **Preheat Oven:** Preheat to 375°F (190°C) and grease a muffin tin.
2. **Mix Ingredients:** In a bowl, whisk eggs, vegetables, cheese, salt, and pepper.
3. **Bake:** Pour the mixture into the muffin cups and bake for 15-20 minutes or until set.
4. **Serve:** Let cool slightly before removing from the tin.

Hummus and Veggie Wrap

Ingredients:

- 2 large tortillas
- 4 tablespoons hummus
- 1/2 cup shredded carrots
- 1/2 cup cucumber slices
- 1/2 cup spinach leaves

Instructions:

1. **Spread Hummus:** Spread hummus evenly on each tortilla.
2. **Add Vegetables:** Layer carrots, cucumber, and spinach on top.
3. **Roll and Serve:** Roll tightly, slice in half, and serve.

Tuna Salad

Ingredients:

- 1 can tuna (drained)
- 2 tablespoons mayonnaise
- 1/4 cup diced celery
- 1/4 teaspoon salt
- 1/4 teaspoon pepper

Instructions:

1. **Mix Ingredients:** In a bowl, combine tuna, mayonnaise, celery, salt, and pepper.
2. **Serve:** Serve on bread, crackers, or a bed of lettuce.

Avocado and Tomato Sandwich

Ingredients:

- 2 slices of whole-grain bread
- 1/2 avocado (sliced)
- 1/2 cup tomato slices
- Salt and pepper to taste

Instructions:

1. **Toast Bread (Optional):** Lightly toast the bread for extra texture.
2. **Assemble Sandwich:** Layer avocado and tomato slices on one slice of bread. Sprinkle with salt and pepper.
3. **Serve:** Top with the second slice of bread, cut in half, and serve.

Turkey and Cheese Roll-Ups

Ingredients:

- 4 slices turkey breast
- 4 slices cheese (e.g., Swiss or cheddar)
- 4 lettuce leaves

Instructions:

1. **Assemble Roll-Ups:** Lay a turkey slice flat, place a cheese slice and a lettuce leaf on top, then roll tightly.
2. **Serve:** Slice in half if desired and serve as a snack or light lunch.

Pesto Pasta

Ingredients:

- 2 cups cooked pasta
- 1/4 cup basil pesto
- 1/4 cup grated Parmesan cheese
- Optional: Cherry tomatoes and pine nuts for garnish

Instructions:

1. **Mix Pasta and Pesto:** Toss the cooked pasta with pesto until evenly coated.
2. **Add Garnish:** Sprinkle with Parmesan cheese and optional toppings.
3. **Serve:** Serve warm or cold.

Smashed Chickpea Salad Sandwich

Ingredients:

- 1 can chickpeas (drained and rinsed)
- 2 tablespoons mayonnaise or Greek yogurt
- 1 teaspoon Dijon mustard
- 1/4 cup diced celery
- 1/4 teaspoon garlic powder
- Salt and pepper to taste
- 4 slices whole-grain bread

Instructions:

1. **Mash Chickpeas:** In a bowl, mash the chickpeas with a fork until mostly smooth.
2. **Mix Salad:** Add mayonnaise or yogurt, mustard, celery, garlic powder, salt, and pepper. Mix well.
3. **Assemble Sandwich:** Spread the mixture onto bread slices, top with your preferred veggies (e.g., lettuce or tomatoes), and close the sandwich.

Apple and Peanut Butter Slices

Ingredients:

- 1 apple (sliced)
- 2 tablespoons peanut butter
- Optional: Granola or chocolate chips for topping

Instructions:

1. **Prepare Apple:** Slice the apple into wedges.
2. **Add Peanut Butter:** Spread peanut butter on each apple slice.
3. **Garnish:** Sprinkle with granola or chocolate chips if desired.

Chicken Salad Lettuce Wraps

Ingredients:

- 1 cup cooked chicken (shredded)
- 2 tablespoons mayonnaise or Greek yogurt
- 1/4 cup diced celery
- 1/4 cup diced grapes or apples
- 4 large lettuce leaves

Instructions:

1. **Make Chicken Salad:** In a bowl, combine chicken, mayonnaise, celery, and fruit. Mix well.
2. **Assemble Wraps:** Spoon the chicken salad into lettuce leaves.
3. **Serve:** Fold the lettuce around the filling and serve as wraps.

Veggie and Cream Cheese Roll-Ups

Ingredients:

- 2 large tortillas
- 4 tablespoons cream cheese
- 1/2 cup shredded carrots
- 1/2 cup cucumber slices
- 1/2 cup bell pepper strips

Instructions:

1. **Spread Cream Cheese:** Evenly spread cream cheese over each tortilla.
2. **Add Vegetables:** Layer carrots, cucumbers, and peppers on top.
3. **Roll and Slice:** Roll tightly and slice into pinwheels.

Bento Box with Rice, Veggies, and Fruit

Ingredients:

- 1 cup cooked rice
- 1/2 cup steamed broccoli
- 1/4 cup cherry tomatoes
- 1/4 cup sliced fruit (e.g., apple, orange)
- 2 tablespoons soy sauce (optional)

Instructions:

1. **Assemble Bento Box:** Arrange rice, broccoli, tomatoes, and fruit in a container.
2. **Optional:** Add a small container of soy sauce for dipping.

Mini Meatballs and Marinara

Ingredients:

- 1/2 pound ground beef or turkey
- 1/4 cup breadcrumbs
- 1 egg
- 1/4 teaspoon garlic powder
- 1/2 cup marinara sauce

Instructions:

1. **Make Meatballs:** Combine ground meat, breadcrumbs, egg, and garlic powder in a bowl. Roll into small balls.
2. **Cook Meatballs:** Bake or pan-fry meatballs until cooked through.
3. **Serve with Marinara:** Heat marinara sauce and pour over the meatballs before serving.

Sweet Potato and Black Bean Burrito

Ingredients:

- 1 medium sweet potato (diced and roasted)
- 1/2 cup black beans
- 1/4 cup salsa
- 1/4 cup shredded cheese
- 2 large tortillas

Instructions:

1. **Prepare Filling:** Mix roasted sweet potato, black beans, salsa, and cheese.
2. **Assemble Burrito:** Place the filling in the center of each tortilla, fold, and roll tightly.
3. **Serve:** Warm in a skillet or microwave before serving.

Baked Chicken Tenders

Ingredients:

- 1 pound chicken tenders
- 1/2 cup breadcrumbs
- 1/4 cup grated Parmesan cheese
- 1 egg (beaten)
- Salt and pepper to taste

Instructions:

1. **Preheat Oven:** Preheat to 400°F (200°C) and line a baking sheet with parchment paper.
2. **Coat Chicken:** Dip each chicken tender in egg, then in a mixture of breadcrumbs, Parmesan, salt, and pepper.
3. **Bake:** Place on the baking sheet and bake for 15-20 minutes or until golden brown and cooked through.

Spinach and Feta Wrap

Ingredients:

- 1 large tortilla
- 1/2 cup fresh spinach leaves
- 1/4 cup crumbled feta cheese
- 1 tablespoon hummus (optional)

Instructions:

1. **Spread Hummus:** If desired, spread hummus over the tortilla.
2. **Add Spinach and Feta:** Layer spinach leaves and sprinkle feta cheese on top.
3. **Roll and Serve:** Roll tightly and slice in half to serve.

Fruit Salad with Yogurt

Ingredients:

- 1 cup mixed fruit (e.g., berries, apple slices, banana, orange segments)
- 1/2 cup Greek yogurt
- 1 teaspoon honey or maple syrup (optional)

Instructions:

1. **Prepare Fruit:** Chop fruit into bite-sized pieces and combine in a bowl.
2. **Add Yogurt:** Top with Greek yogurt and drizzle with honey or maple syrup if desired.
3. **Mix and Serve:** Toss gently and serve chilled.

Mini Pizzas

Ingredients:

- 4 English muffin halves or small pita rounds
- 1/2 cup marinara sauce
- 1/2 cup shredded mozzarella cheese
- Toppings of choice (e.g., pepperoni, veggies)

Instructions:

1. **Preheat Oven:** Preheat to 375°F (190°C).
2. **Assemble Pizzas:** Spread marinara sauce on each muffin half or pita. Add cheese and toppings.
3. **Bake:** Place on a baking sheet and bake for 8-10 minutes until cheese melts.

Chicken and Veggie Skewers

Ingredients:

- 1 cup cubed chicken breast
- 1 cup mixed veggies (e.g., bell peppers, zucchini, cherry tomatoes)
- 1 tablespoon olive oil
- Salt, pepper, and seasoning of choice

Instructions:

1. **Prepare Skewers:** Thread chicken and veggies onto skewers.
2. **Season:** Drizzle with olive oil and sprinkle with seasonings.
3. **Cook:** Grill or bake at 375°F (190°C) for 15-20 minutes until chicken is cooked through.

Roasted Veggie and Quinoa Bowl

Ingredients:

- 1 cup cooked quinoa
- 1 cup roasted vegetables (e.g., sweet potatoes, zucchini, carrots)
- 1 tablespoon olive oil
- 1 tablespoon tahini or dressing of choice

Instructions:

1. **Roast Veggies:** Toss vegetables in olive oil, roast at 400°F (200°C) for 20 minutes.
2. **Assemble Bowl:** Place quinoa in a bowl, top with roasted veggies.
3. **Drizzle Dressing:** Add tahini or dressing before serving.

Almond Butter and Banana Sandwich

Ingredients:

- 2 slices whole-grain bread
- 2 tablespoons almond butter
- 1 banana (sliced)

Instructions:

1. **Spread Almond Butter:** Spread almond butter evenly on one side of each bread slice.
2. **Add Banana Slices:** Place banana slices on one slice of bread.
3. **Assemble Sandwich:** Close the sandwich and serve as is or grilled.

Shrimp and Avocado Salad

Ingredients:

- 1 cup cooked shrimp
- 1/2 avocado (cubed)
- 1 cup mixed greens
- 1 tablespoon olive oil
- 1 teaspoon lemon juice
- Salt and pepper to taste

Instructions:

1. **Prepare Salad:** Combine shrimp, avocado, and greens in a bowl.
2. **Add Dressing:** Drizzle with olive oil and lemon juice, then season with salt and pepper.
3. **Toss and Serve:** Mix gently and serve immediately.

Grilled Cheese and Tomato Soup

Ingredients for Grilled Cheese:

- 2 slices bread
- 2 slices cheddar cheese
- 1 tablespoon butter

Ingredients for Tomato Soup:

- 1 cup canned tomato puree
- 1/2 cup vegetable broth
- 1/4 teaspoon garlic powder
- 1 tablespoon cream (optional)

Instructions for Grilled Cheese:

1. **Assemble Sandwich:** Place cheese between slices of bread.
2. **Grill:** Heat butter in a skillet and cook the sandwich on both sides until golden brown.

Instructions for Tomato Soup:

1. **Simmer:** Heat tomato puree, broth, and garlic powder in a saucepan.
2. **Add Cream:** Stir in cream if desired, then serve with the grilled cheese.

Veggie Stir-Fry with Tofu

Ingredients:

- 1 cup firm tofu (cubed)
- 1 cup mixed veggies (e.g., broccoli, carrots, bell peppers)
- 1 tablespoon soy sauce
- 1 teaspoon sesame oil
- 1 teaspoon minced garlic

Instructions:

1. **Cook Tofu:** Sauté tofu in a skillet until golden, then set aside.
2. **Stir-Fry Veggies:** In the same skillet, cook veggies with garlic and sesame oil.
3. **Combine:** Return tofu to the skillet, add soy sauce, and toss well before serving.

Pulled Pork Sliders

Ingredients:

- 2 cups cooked pulled pork
- 1/2 cup barbecue sauce
- 8 slider buns
- Pickles or coleslaw (optional)

Instructions:

1. **Prepare Pork:** Mix pulled pork with barbecue sauce in a skillet and heat through.
2. **Assemble Sliders:** Place pork on slider buns, add pickles or coleslaw if desired.
3. **Serve:** Serve warm.

Eggplant Parmesan Bites

Ingredients:

- 1 medium eggplant (cubed)
- 1/2 cup breadcrumbs
- 1/4 cup grated Parmesan cheese
- 1 egg (beaten)
- Marinara sauce (for dipping)

Instructions:

1. **Preheat Oven:** Set to 400°F (200°C).
2. **Coat Eggplant:** Dip eggplant cubes in egg, then coat with a breadcrumb and Parmesan mixture.
3. **Bake:** Place on a baking sheet and bake for 20 minutes until crispy. Serve with marinara sauce.

Salmon Salad

Ingredients:

- 1 cup cooked salmon (flaked)
- 1/4 cup Greek yogurt or mayo
- 1 teaspoon lemon juice
- 1 tablespoon chopped dill
- Salt and pepper to taste

Instructions:

1. **Combine Ingredients:** Mix salmon, yogurt or mayo, lemon juice, dill, salt, and pepper.
2. **Serve:** Serve on crackers, bread, or lettuce leaves.

Whole Wheat Pita with Cucumber and Yogurt

Ingredients:

- 1 whole wheat pita
- 1/2 cup diced cucumber
- 1/4 cup plain yogurt
- 1 teaspoon olive oil
- Salt and pepper to taste

Instructions:

1. **Prepare Yogurt Spread:** Mix yogurt with olive oil, salt, and pepper.
2. **Assemble:** Spread yogurt on pita, top with diced cucumber.
3. **Serve:** Fold and serve immediately.

Apple and Cheese Slices

Ingredients:

- 1 apple (sliced)
- 1/4 cup sliced cheddar cheese

Instructions:

1. **Slice Apple and Cheese:** Cut apple and cheese into thin slices.
2. **Serve:** Arrange alternately on a plate for an easy snack.

Chicken Lettuce Cups

Ingredients:

- 1 cup cooked chicken (shredded)
- 1/4 cup hoisin sauce or soy sauce
- 8 lettuce leaves (e.g., romaine or butter lettuce)
- Optional toppings: chopped peanuts, green onions

Instructions:

1. **Prepare Filling:** Mix chicken with hoisin or soy sauce.
2. **Assemble:** Spoon chicken mixture into lettuce leaves and top with optional toppings.
3. **Serve:** Serve as finger food.

Zucchini Fritters

Ingredients:

- 2 cups shredded zucchini
- 1/4 cup flour
- 1 egg (beaten)
- 1/4 cup grated Parmesan cheese
- Salt and pepper to taste
- Olive oil for frying

Instructions:

1. **Prepare Zucchini:** Squeeze out excess water from shredded zucchini.
2. **Mix Ingredients:** Combine zucchini, flour, egg, Parmesan, salt, and pepper.
3. **Fry:** Heat olive oil in a skillet, drop spoonfuls of the mixture, and flatten slightly. Cook 2-3 minutes per side until golden.

Veggie Sushi Rolls

Ingredients:

- 1 cup cooked sushi rice
- 4 nori sheets
- Thinly sliced veggies (e.g., cucumber, carrot, avocado)
- Soy sauce (for dipping)

Instructions:

1. **Prepare Rice:** Spread a thin layer of sushi rice on nori sheets.
2. **Add Veggies:** Place sliced veggies in a line near one edge.
3. **Roll:** Roll tightly and slice into pieces. Serve with soy sauce.

Roasted Chickpeas and Veggies

Ingredients:

- 1 cup canned chickpeas (drained and rinsed)
- 1 cup mixed veggies (e.g., broccoli, carrots, bell peppers)
- 1 tablespoon olive oil
- 1 teaspoon smoked paprika or seasoning of choice
- Salt and pepper to taste

Instructions:

1. **Preheat Oven:** Set to 400°F (200°C).
2. **Combine Ingredients:** Toss chickpeas and veggies with olive oil and seasonings.
3. **Roast:** Spread on a baking sheet and roast for 20-25 minutes until crispy.

Cottage Cheese with Fruit

Ingredients:

- 1 cup cottage cheese
- 1/2 cup fresh fruit (e.g., berries, pineapple, peaches)
- 1 teaspoon honey or maple syrup (optional)
- A sprinkle of granola or nuts (optional)

Instructions:

1. **Assemble:** Scoop cottage cheese into a bowl and top with fresh fruit.
2. **Optional Additions:** Drizzle with honey or sprinkle with granola/nuts for added texture and flavor.
3. **Serve:** Enjoy chilled.

Carrot and Cucumber Sticks with Dip

Ingredients:

- 2 carrots (cut into sticks)
- 1 cucumber (cut into sticks)
- 1/2 cup hummus or ranch dressing (for dipping)

Instructions:

1. **Prepare Vegetables:** Cut carrots and cucumbers into sticks or slices.
2. **Serve:** Arrange on a plate with the dip in the center.

Avocado and Bean Wrap

Ingredients:

- 1 large tortilla or flatbread
- 1/2 avocado (sliced or mashed)
- 1/2 cup black beans (rinsed and drained)
- 1/4 cup shredded lettuce or spinach
- 1 tablespoon salsa or hot sauce (optional)

Instructions:

1. **Assemble Wrap:** Spread avocado onto the tortilla, layer beans, greens, and optional salsa.
2. **Wrap:** Roll tightly and slice in half for easier eating.
3. **Serve:** Enjoy as a light meal or snack.

Turkey and Spinach Pinwheels

Ingredients:

- 4 large tortillas
- 8 slices of deli turkey
- 1 cup fresh spinach leaves
- 1/4 cup cream cheese (softened)

Instructions:

1. **Spread Cream Cheese:** Evenly spread cream cheese over each tortilla.
2. **Layer Fillings:** Add slices of turkey and spinach leaves.
3. **Roll and Slice:** Roll tightly and slice into 1-inch pieces to form pinwheels.

Pasta with Pesto and Veggies

Ingredients:

- 2 cups cooked pasta (e.g., penne, rotini)
- 1/4 cup pesto sauce
- 1 cup mixed veggies (e.g., cherry tomatoes, zucchini, bell peppers)
- Grated Parmesan cheese (optional)

Instructions:

1. **Cook Veggies:** Sauté veggies in olive oil until tender.
2. **Mix Pasta and Pesto:** Toss cooked pasta with pesto sauce.
3. **Combine:** Add sautéed veggies to the pasta and mix well.
4. **Serve:** Garnish with Parmesan if desired.

www.ingramcontent.com/pod-product-compliance
Lightning Source LLC
LaVergne TN
LVHW061955070526
838199LV00060B/4140